Supply Chain Leadership Mastery:

Crafting High-Performing Winning Teams

Table of Contents:

Introduction:

In the ever-evolving world of supply chain and logistics, where precision, efficiency, and adaptability are paramount, leadership is the linchpin that can turn an ordinary team into an extraordinary one. The complex tapestry of global commerce relies on the skilled hands and sharp minds of supply chain and logistics professionals, and at the heart of this intricate web stands a leader—a leader with the vision to steer the course, the wisdom to adapt to change, and the ability to build and nurture a high-performing winning team.

Welcome to "Supply Chain Leadership Mastery: Crafting High-Performing Winning Teams." This book is your comprehensive guide to becoming an exceptional leader in the supply chain and logistics industry, where success hinges not only on the movement of goods but also on the cultivation of talent, the pursuit of innovation, and the stewardship of sustainability.

The journey of supply chain and logistics leadership is a rewarding yet demanding one. It requires a deep understanding of the industry's dynamics, the ability to navigate uncertainty, and the skill to inspire and motivate a diverse team of professionals who orchestrate the movement of goods across the globe. It's a journey that is both an art and a science, blending the artistry of leadership with the science of logistics.

In the chapters that follow, we will delve into the core principles, strategies, and best practices that underpin the creation of high-performing winning teams in the supply chain and logistics world. We will explore the nuances of effective leadership, from crafting a compelling vision to setting ambitious goals and leading by example. We will also investigate the critical components of building and nurturing teams, from talent acquisition and training to fostering collaboration and embracing diversity.

Furthermore, we will uncover the secrets of performance optimization, utilizing key performance indicators (KPIs), leveraging technology and automation, managing risks, and embracing sustainability as a cornerstone of modern logistics leadership.

Change is an ever-present force in our industry, and we will equip you with the tools to not only navigate change but to thrive in it. We will explore the art of innovation and provide insights into emerging trends and technologies that will shape the future of supply chain and logistics.

This book is not just a theoretical guide; it is a practical manual filled with real-world examples, actionable insights, and valuable strategies that will empower you to lead with confidence, inspire your team, and achieve supply chain excellence. Whether you are a seasoned industry veteran or a newcomer eager to make your mark, the principles and knowledge within these pages will propel you toward your leadership aspirations.

The world of supply chain and logistics is ever in motion, and so too must be our approach to leadership. Join us on this journey as we embark on the quest for supply chain leadership mastery, and let us work together to craft high-performing winning teams that will shape the future of our industry.

Chapter 1: Understanding the Supply Chain and Logistics Landscape

The Importance of Supply Chain and Logistics

Supply chain and logistics are the unseen engines that power the global economy. In an era marked by rapid technological advancement, interconnected markets, and evolving consumer demands, the efficient management of these processes has become paramount. This chapter unveils the profound significance of supply chain and logistics in modern business operations, shedding light on their far-reaching impact on customer satisfaction, cost management, and overall competitiveness.

The Heartbeat of Commerce

Imagine a world without supply chains and logistics. Products wouldn't reach store shelves, online orders would remain unfulfilled, and industries would grind to a halt. Supply chain and logistics serve as the beating heart of commerce, facilitating the movement of raw materials, components, and finished goods across vast geographic distances.

At its core, the supply chain encompasses a series of interrelated activities, including sourcing raw materials, manufacturing, transportation, warehousing, distribution, and delivery to end customers. It is a complex, interconnected network that spans continents, involving numerous stakeholders, from suppliers and manufacturers to distributors and retailers.

The logistics component of this process is equally critical. Logistics deals with the planning, execution, and management of the physical flow of goods, from their point of origin to their final destination. It encompasses everything from inventory management and transportation to order fulfillment and reverse logistics (the process of handling returns).

Customer Satisfaction as the North Star

In a competitive marketplace, meeting and exceeding customer expectations is a top priority. Customers today are not only looking for high-quality products but also seamless, efficient, and timely service. This is where supply chain and logistics come into play.

A well-optimized supply chain ensures that products are available when and where customers want them. It minimizes delays, stockouts, and other disruptions that can lead to customer dissatisfaction. Furthermore, effective logistics management ensures that products are delivered promptly and in pristine condition, enhancing the overall customer experience.

Consider the e-commerce sector as an illustrative example. Amazon, the e-commerce giant, is renowned for its logistics prowess. The company's ability to deliver products to customers' doorsteps in record time has set a new standard for customer expectations. This exceptional logistics performance has not only boosted customer satisfaction but also fueled Amazon's meteoric rise.

Cost Management and Competitiveness

In addition to customer satisfaction, supply chain and logistics play a pivotal role in cost management and overall competitiveness. Effective supply chain management can lead to significant cost savings by streamlining processes, reducing waste, and optimizing inventory. It allows companies to operate more efficiently, translating into a competitive advantage.

Conversely, a poorly managed supply chain can result in inefficiencies, excess costs, and missed opportunities. The failure to deliver products to market on time can lead to lost sales, while excessive inventory holdings can tie up valuable capital. Thus, the financial health and profitability of a business are intricately linked to the effectiveness of its supply chain and logistics operations.

The Global Supply Chain Web

The modern supply chain is a global web of interconnected activities. Raw materials sourced from one corner of the world are transformed into finished products in another, then transported to yet another region for distribution. This global reach offers both opportunities and challenges.

On the one hand, it opens up access to a vast array of resources, markets, and talent pools. Companies can tap into specialized suppliers, reach a global customer base, and benefit from economies of scale. However, this global complexity also introduces risks, such as supply chain disruptions, geopolitical tensions, and regulatory compliance issues.

In essence, the importance of supply chain and logistics extends far beyond the confines of any single company. It is an ecosystem in which businesses operate, collaborate, and compete. Understanding this ecosystem is the first step towards mastering supply chain leadership.

Evolving Industry Trends

The supply chain and logistics landscape is a dynamic arena where change is not only constant but also accelerating. Emerging technologies, shifting market dynamics, and evolving consumer preferences are reshaping the industry in profound ways. To thrive as a leader in this environment, it is imperative to not only recognize these trends but also harness them for competitive advantage. In this section, we embark on a journey into the key trends that are propelling the industry forward.

The Rise of E-Commerce

The advent of e-commerce has revolutionized the way consumers shop, creating a seismic shift in supply chain and logistics practices. The convenience of online shopping has driven an exponential increase in the volume of goods being shipped directly to consumers' homes. As a result, supply chains are adapting to accommodate the unique demands of e-commerce, such as rapid order fulfillment, last-mile delivery, and an increased focus on customer experience.

Automation and Robotics

Automation and robotics are transforming the warehouse and distribution center landscape. Robots are being used for tasks ranging from picking and packing to material handling and inventory management. Autonomous vehicles, including drones and self-driving trucks, are poised to revolutionize transportation, offering increased efficiency and reduced costs. These technologies are not just on the horizon; they are already reshaping the industry's operations.

Big Data and Analytics

Data is the new currency of supply chain and logistics. The industry is increasingly relying on big data and advanced analytics to gain insights, optimize operations, and enhance decision-making. Predictive analytics can help forecast demand more accurately, while real-time data analysis can improve supply chain visibility and responsiveness.

Sustainability and Green Logistics

Sustainability is no longer a mere buzzword; it has become a critical imperative in supply chain and logistics. Consumers and regulators are demanding greater environmental responsibility, prompting companies to adopt eco-friendly practices. This includes reducing carbon emissions, minimizing waste, and exploring alternative energy sources. Sustainability is not only a moral obligation but also a source of cost savings and competitive advantage.

Supply Chain Resilience

In an era marked by natural disasters, global disruptions, and unforeseen challenges (as demonstrated by the COVID-19 pandemic), supply chain resilience has emerged as a key focus area. Companies are investing in strategies to enhance their ability to withstand and recover from disruptions. This includes diversifying supply sources, implementing robust risk management practices, and creating contingency plans.

The Internet of Things (IoT)

The Internet of Things (IoT) is connecting physical objects to the digital world, creating new opportunities for supply chain optimization. IoT sensors can track the condition, location, and status of goods in real-time, providing unprecedented visibility and control. This technology is being used for everything from monitoring temperature-sensitive pharmaceuticals to tracking the movement of shipping containers across the globe.

Supply Chain Collaboration

Collaboration is emerging as a driving force in supply chain and logistics. Companies are realizing that working together with suppliers, partners, and even competitors can lead to mutually beneficial outcomes. Collaborative supply chain networks are becoming more common, allowing for shared resources, information, and expertise.

Regulatory Changes

Regulatory changes and geopolitical factors can have a profound impact on supply chain and logistics operations. Tariffs, trade agreements, and customs regulations can disrupt global supply chains, necessitating agile responses. Staying informed and adaptable in the face of regulatory shifts is crucial for supply chain leaders.

Leaner and Greener Supply Chains

Efficiency and sustainability are no longer at odds. Companies are increasingly adopting lean principles to reduce waste and enhance efficiency while simultaneously minimizing their environmental footprint. Lean practices, combined with sustainability initiatives, are yielding dual benefits: cost savings and environmental stewardship.

The Human Element

Amidst all the technological advancements, the human element remains indispensable. The industry requires skilled professionals who can harness technology, make strategic decisions, and collaborate effectively. Leadership and talent development will continue to be critical aspects of supply chain and logistics excellence.

In the following chapters, we will delve deeper into these trends, exploring their implications and providing strategies for supply chain leaders to navigate and leverage them effectively. Understanding these trends is not just a matter of staying current;

it is essential for building high-performing, future-ready supply chain teams.

This concludes the content for Chapter 1. In the subsequent chapters, we will continue to explore the multifaceted world of supply chain and logistics leadership.

Chapter 2: Leadership Foundations

The Role of Leadership in Supply Chain Excellence

In the intricate dance of global supply chains, leadership takes center stage. Effective leaders serve as the architects of supply chain excellence, guiding their teams through the complexities of modern logistics, and ensuring the seamless flow of goods and information. This chapter explores the pivotal role that leadership plays in ensuring the smooth and efficient operation of supply chains. It examines how leaders serve as the linchpin between strategy and execution, setting the tone for success.

The Link Between Leadership and Supply Chain Excellence

Supply chain excellence is not a happy accident but the result of deliberate leadership. The supply chain ecosystem is vast, encompassing numerous stakeholders, from suppliers and manufacturers to distributors and retailers. Navigating this complex web requires strong leadership to coordinate activities, make strategic decisions, and steer the ship towards a common goal.

Leadership in supply chain management is not solely about making decisions; it's about making the right decisions that align with the organization's overarching objectives. Effective leaders in the supply chain and logistics field are those who can see the bigger picture, anticipate challenges, and chart a course that leads to competitive advantage.

From Strategy to Execution

One of the distinguishing features of supply chain leadership is the ability to bridge the gap between strategic vision and practical execution. A well-crafted supply chain strategy is meaningless without effective execution, and this is where leadership comes into play.

Leaders must translate high-level strategic goals into actionable plans, ensuring that every member of the team understands their role in achieving these objectives. They are responsible for aligning the supply chain's activities with the company's broader mission and vision, creating a sense of purpose that energizes the team.

The Power of Alignment

Alignment is a critical facet of leadership in supply chain management. It involves harmonizing the goals, processes, and activities of different departments and functions within an organization. When supply chain leaders align their strategies with other business units, they create a unified front that drives efficiency and success.

For example, a supply chain leader may work closely with the marketing team to ensure that the supply chain can respond effectively to changes in demand resulting from marketing campaigns. This alignment not only prevents disruptions but also capitalizes on opportunities for growth.

Defining Leadership in Logistics

Leadership in logistics is a specialized field that requires a unique set of skills and attributes. It's about more than just guiding a team; it's about navigating the intricacies of the logistics landscape, making informed decisions in the face of complexity, and driving continuous improvement.

The Logistics Leader's Role

At the heart of logistics leadership is the responsibility to ensure the smooth and efficient movement of goods from point A to point B.

This involves overseeing a wide range of activities, from transportation and warehousing to inventory management and order fulfillment.

Logistics leaders are tasked with optimizing the entire logistics chain. They must make decisions about the most cost-effective transportation routes, warehouse layouts, inventory levels, and distribution strategies. The ability to manage these factors effectively is central to their role.

The Need for a Deep Understanding

A key characteristic of logistics leaders is their deep understanding of the logistics processes. They are well-versed in the intricacies of supply chain management, from procurement and production to distribution and delivery. This knowledge enables them to make informed decisions and identify opportunities for improvement.

In a world where logistics can be a source of competitive advantage, logistics leaders must be able to speak the language of supply chain efficiency. They understand the significance of on-time deliveries, optimal inventory levels, and streamlined processes.

Making Sound Decisions in Complexity

Logistics is inherently complex, with multiple variables and moving parts. Effective logistics leaders thrive in this complexity. They can synthesize vast amounts of data, anticipate potential bottlenecks, and make decisions that keep the supply chain flowing smoothly.

These decisions may involve choosing the right transportation mode, negotiating with carriers, optimizing route planning, and managing inventory effectively. Each decision has a ripple effect throughout the supply chain, underscoring the importance of thoughtful, informed leadership.

Leadership Styles in the Industry

Leadership is not a one-size-fits-all proposition; it comes in various styles, each with its unique strengths and approaches. In the supply chain and logistics industry, leaders must adapt their style to different situations and team dynamics. This section explores different leadership styles commonly found in the industry, shedding light on when and how to apply them.

Transformational Leadership

Transformational leaders are visionaries who inspire and motivate their teams by articulating a compelling vision of the future. They encourage creativity and innovation, challenging the status quo and driving change. In the supply chain context, transformational leaders might champion the adoption of new technologies or processes that revolutionize logistics operations.

Transactional Leadership

Transactional leaders focus on establishing clear structures and processes. They emphasize the importance of compliance with established standards and procedures. In logistics, this style can be beneficial for ensuring consistency and reliability in day-to-day operations. Transactional leaders may use performance metrics and incentives to drive results.

Servant Leadership

Servant leaders prioritize the well-being and development of their team members. They lead by serving others, aiming to empower individuals to reach their full potential. In the supply chain, this style can foster a culture of collaboration and continuous improvement. Servant leaders support their team members and remove obstacles in their path.

Situational Leadership

Situational leaders adapt their leadership style to match the specific needs of a situation or team member. They recognize that different challenges and individuals require different approaches. In logistics, situational leaders might provide guidance to a team dealing with a sudden disruption while allowing a well-established team to work autonomously.

Adaptive Leadership

Adaptive leaders thrive in dynamic, uncertain environments. They are flexible and responsive, capable of adjusting their strategies as circumstances change. In the fast-paced world of supply chain and logistics, adaptive leaders excel at navigating disruptions, making quick decisions, and leading their teams through change.

Collaborative Leadership

Collaborative leaders prioritize teamwork and understand that the success of any endeavor is often a collective achievement, and they prioritize teamwork as a cornerstone of their leadership philosophy. These leaders recognize that when individuals with diverse skills, experiences, and perspectives come together, they can achieve more than any one person can on their own. They foster an environment where open communication, trust, and cooperation are not just encouraged but actively cultivated. By valuing and promoting teamwork, collaborative leaders harness the collective potential of their team, driving innovation, problem-solving, and overall organizational success. Their commitment to working together as a cohesive unit not only strengthens bonds among team members but also inspires a shared sense of purpose that propels their group towards achieving common goals.

Chapter 3: Vision, Strategy, and Goal Setting - Leading by Example

In the intricate world of supply chain leadership, a well-crafted vision, strategic planning, and effective goal setting are the guiding stars that illuminate the path to success. This chapter explores the art of crafting a compelling vision, developing strategic plans, and setting SMART (Specific, Measurable, Achievable, Relevant, Time-bound) goals for your supply chain team. It underscores the importance of leading by example, building trust and credibility, and upholding ethical leadership in logistics.

Crafting a Vision for Supply Chain Success

A compelling vision is the cornerstone of supply chain leadership. It serves as the beacon that guides your team's efforts, providing direction, inspiration, and purpose. Crafting a vision for supply chain success requires a delicate blend of foresight, communication skills, and an intimate understanding of your organization's mission and values.

The Power of Vision

A well-defined vision statement encapsulates your aspirations for the supply chain and logistics operations. It should be concise, memorable, and future-oriented. A compelling vision has the power to inspire and rally your team, aligning their efforts with the overarching goals of the organization.

Elements of a Compelling Vision

1. **Clarity:** A clear and concise vision statement leaves no room for ambiguity. It should be easy for every team member to understand and embrace.

2. **Inspiration:** A vision should evoke excitement and a sense of purpose. It should ignite the passion and dedication of your team, motivating them to work towards a common goal.

3. **Alignment:** The vision must align with the broader objectives and values of the organization. It should harmonize with the company's mission and resonate with stakeholders.

4. **Realism:** While a vision should be aspirational, it should also be grounded in reality. Unrealistic or unattainable visions can lead to frustration and disillusionment.

Practical Tips for Crafting a Vision

1. **Involve Your Team:** Engage your team in the vision-crafting process. Encourage them to share their ideas and perspectives. A collective vision is more likely to be embraced and pursued.

2. **Consider the Long Term:** A vision should extend beyond short-term goals. Think about where you want your supply chain team to be in three, five, or even ten years.

3. **Communicate Effectively:** Once you've crafted a vision, communicate it consistently and passionately. Use various channels to ensure that every team member is aware of and aligned with the vision.

4. **Measure Progress:** Establish key performance indicators (KPIs) that can help you measure progress towards your vision. Regularly assess and communicate these metrics to track your team's success.

Developing Strategic Plans

A compelling vision sets the destination, but a strategic plan is the roadmap that guides you there. Strategic planning is the process of translating your vision into actionable goals and initiatives. It involves assessing your strengths, weaknesses, opportunities, and threats (SWOT analysis), identifying strategic priorities, and creating a detailed plan for achieving your objectives.

The Strategic Planning Process

1. **SWOT Analysis:** Begin by conducting a comprehensive SWOT analysis of your supply chain and logistics operations. Identify internal strengths and weaknesses as well as external opportunities and threats.

2. **Goal Setting:** Based on the insights from your SWOT analysis, set clear and specific goals that align with your vision. These goals should be the building blocks of your strategic plan.

3. **Actionable Initiatives:** Break down each goal into actionable initiatives or projects. Assign responsibilities, set deadlines, and establish performance metrics for each initiative.

4. **Resource Allocation:** Determine the resources—financial, human, and technological—that will be required to execute your strategic plan successfully. Allocate resources strategically to support your initiatives.

5. **Risk Assessment:** Identify potential risks and challenges that could impede the achievement of your goals. Develop contingency plans to mitigate these risks.

6. **Monitoring and Evaluation:** Implement a system for monitoring progress and evaluating the effectiveness of your strategic plan. Regularly review your KPIs and make adjustments as necessary.

Benefits of Strategic Planning

Strategic planning in the supply chain and logistics context offers several advantages:

- **Alignment:** It ensures that your team's efforts are aligned with your vision and organizational goals.

- **Efficiency:** By identifying strategic priorities and allocating resources effectively, you can streamline operations and reduce waste.

- **Adaptability:** A well-structured plan allows your team to adapt to changing market conditions and seize emerging opportunities.

- **Accountability:** Clear goals and responsibilities enhance accountability within your team, fostering a results-oriented culture.

Setting SMART Goals for Your Team

Goals are the stepping stones that lead to your vision's realization. To ensure that your team's objectives are clear, achievable, and aligned with the broader strategic plan, it's essential to apply the SMART framework to goal setting.

Specific

Specific goals are well-defined and clear. They leave no room for ambiguity. Instead of setting a vague goal like "improve supply chain efficiency," a specific goal would be "reduce order processing time by 20% within six months." This specificity provides a clear target for your team to aim for.

Measurable

Measurable goals are quantifiable and allow for tracking progress. You should be able to determine whether or not a goal has been achieved based on concrete metrics. For example, if your goal is to increase on-time deliveries, you can measure success by tracking the percentage of orders delivered on time.

Achievable

Achievable goals are realistic and attainable within the given constraints. While it's important to set ambitious goals, they should also be within the realm of possibility. Setting unattainable goals can lead to frustration and demotivation within your team.

Relevant

Relevant goals are aligned with your team's and organization's objectives. Each goal should contribute to the broader mission and vision. Avoid setting goals that are unrelated or contradictory to your vision and strategic plan.

Time-Bound

Time-bound goals have a specific deadline or timeframe for completion. This element adds a sense of urgency and ensures that your team remains focused on achieving the goal within a defined period. Setting a deadline creates a sense of accountability.

Applying SMART Goals in the Supply Chain

Let's consider an example of setting a SMART goal for your supply chain team:

Specific: Improve supplier lead times for critical components in the manufacturing process.

Measurable: Reduce supplier lead times from an average of 10 days to 5 days.

Achievable: This goal is achievable through negotiations with suppliers and process improvements.

Relevant: Shorter lead times will enhance overall supply chain efficiency and reduce production bottlenecks, aligning with the organization's goals.

Time-Bound: Achieve the reduction in supplier lead times within six months.

SMART goals not only provide clarity but also enable effective performance measurement and progress tracking. They empower your team to work towards well-defined objectives, increasing the likelihood of success.

The Power of Role Modeling

Leadership is not just about what you say; it's about what you do. Your actions, behaviors, and values serve as a model for your team to follow. Leading by example is a powerful way to influence your team's culture, work ethic, and commitment to achieving your vision.

Leading by Example in the Supply Chain

In the supply chain and logistics field, leading by example takes on various forms:

- **Punctuality:** Arriving on time for meetings, deliveries, and other commitments sets a standard of reliability and professionalism.

- **Attention to Detail:** Demonstrating a commitment to accuracy and attention to detail inspires your team to prioritize precision in their work.

- **Communication:** Effective communication, both within your team and with external partners, fosters collaboration and efficiency.

- **Adaptability:** Embracing change and demonstrating a willingness to adapt to new technologies or processes encourages your team to be flexible and open to innovation.

- **Ethical Behavior:** Upholding ethical standards in decision-making and interactions builds trust and sets an ethical tone for your team.

- **Problem-Solving:** Showing a proactive approach to solving problems and addressing challenges inspires your team to seek solutions rather than dwell on issues.

The Impact of Role Modeling

When you lead by example, you create a culture of accountability and excellence within your team. Your actions speak louder than words, reinforcing the values and behaviors you expect from your team members.

Leading by example also fosters trust and credibility. Your team is more likely to respect and trust a leader who practices what they preach. This trust forms the foundation of a strong and cohesive team.

Building Trust and Credibility

Trust is the currency of leadership. It's the foundation upon which successful teams are built. Without trust, collaboration falters, morale suffers, and progress stagnates. Building and maintaining trust within your supply chain team and with key stakeholders is paramount.

Trust within Your Team

1. **Consistency:** Consistency in your actions and decisions builds predictability, which is essential for trust. Team members should know what to expect from their leader.

2. **Open Communication:** Encourage open and honest communication within your team. Actively listen to their concerns and feedback, and address issues promptly.

3. **Transparency:** Be transparent about your decision-making processes and the reasons behind them. Hidden agendas erode trust.

4. **Empowerment:** Trust your team to take ownership of their responsibilities. Empowered team members are more likely to excel and innovate.

5. **Accountability:** Hold yourself and your team accountable for their actions and commitments. When accountability is a shared value, trust flourishes.

Trust with Key Stakeholders

1. **Reliability:** Consistently delivering on your promises and commitments to customers, suppliers, and partners establishes your reliability.

2. **Honesty:** Be forthright in your communications. If challenges or delays arise, communicate them honestly and work collaboratively to find solutions.

3. **Competence:** Demonstrating competence in supply chain management and logistics inspires confidence in your ability to meet expectations.

4. **Responsiveness:** Timely responses to inquiries and issues demonstrate that you prioritize the concerns of your stakeholders.

5. **Consistency:** Consistency in delivering quality products and services reinforces trust over time.

Building trust takes time and effort, but the dividends it pays in team cohesion, collaboration, and performance are immeasurable. Trust is a valuable asset that leaders must continually invest in and protect.

Ethical Leadership in Logistics

Ethical leadership is not a choice but a responsibility in the supply chain and logistics industry. Leaders are entrusted with critical decisions that can impact the lives and well-being of employees, customers, and the broader community. Upholding ethical standards is essential.

Ethical Challenges in Logistics

Logistics leaders may encounter various ethical challenges:

1. **Supplier Relationships:** Ethical concerns may arise when negotiating with suppliers, such as issues related to fair labor practices, environmental responsibility, or quality control.

2. **Sustainability:** Balancing economic goals with sustainability objectives can present ethical dilemmas. Leaders must prioritize environmentally responsible practices.

3. **Data Privacy:** Handling sensitive customer data and ensuring data privacy is an ethical imperative. Data breaches or misuse can result in severe consequences.

4. **Transparency:** Maintaining transparency in business operations and supply chain activities is crucial. Concealing information or engaging in deceptive practices erodes trust.

Making Ethical Decisions

Leaders must be prepared to make ethical decisions even when faced with challenging circumstances. Here are some principles to guide ethical decision-making:

1. **Values Alignment:** Ensure that your decisions align with your organization's values and code of ethics.

2. **Legal Compliance:** Adhere to all relevant laws and regulations. Compliance is the baseline for ethical behavior.

3. **Consider Consequences:** Assess the potential consequences of your decisions on all stakeholders, including employees, customers, and the environment.

4. **Seek Counsel:** If faced with a particularly complex ethical dilemma, seek advice from trusted colleagues, mentors, or ethical experts.

5. **Transparency:** Be transparent about your decision-making process and the ethical considerations involved.

Ethical leadership is not just about avoiding unethical behavior; it's about actively promoting ethical conduct within your team and organization. Upholding ethical standards sets a precedent for your team members to follow.

In conclusion, vision, strategic planning, goal setting, leading by example, and ethical leadership are foundational elements of effective supply chain leadership. They provide the framework for achieving your supply chain objectives while fostering a culture of trust, credibility, and ethical conduct. As a supply chain leader, your role is not only to guide your team toward success but also to inspire them to uphold the highest standards of professionalism and ethics in the complex world of logistics.

Chapter 4: Building a Winning Team - Talent Acquisition and Recruitment

In the world of supply chain leadership, the foundation of success rests upon the strength of your team. Building a high-performing, winning team starts with effective talent acquisition and recruitment. This chapter delves into the essential aspects of assembling a team that can not only meet the demands of today but also anticipate and adapt to the challenges of tomorrow. We will explore talent gap identification, crafting compelling job descriptions, recruitment strategies, team development, onboarding, continuous learning, cross-training, collaboration, communication, and conflict resolution.

Identifying Talent Gaps

The journey to building a winning team begins with a critical examination of your current talent pool and the identification of talent gaps. Understanding where your team falls short in skills, knowledge, or expertise is essential for strategic talent acquisition and development.

Conducting a Skills Audit

A skills audit involves assessing the skills and competencies of your existing team members. This assessment can reveal areas where your team excels and areas that require improvement. Key steps in conducting a skills audit include:

1. **Defining Required Skills:** Identify the skills and competencies needed to excel in various roles within your supply chain team.

2. **Evaluating Current Skills:** Assess the skills of each team member to determine how well they align with the required skills.

3. **Identifying Gaps:** Compare the required skills with the existing skills of your team members to identify gaps.

4. **Prioritizing Development:** Prioritize the development of skills that are critical for achieving your supply chain objectives.

5. **Creating Development Plans:** Work with individual team members to create development plans that address their skill gaps.

6. **Continuous Monitoring:** Regularly review and update the skills audit to ensure your team's skills remain aligned with your goals.

Crafting Compelling Job Descriptions

Crafting job descriptions that attract top talent is a critical step in the recruitment process. A well-crafted job description not only outlines the responsibilities of the role but also showcases your organization's culture and values.

Elements of a Compelling Job Description

1. **Clear Job Title:** The job title should accurately reflect the role's responsibilities and level within the organization.

2. **Responsibilities:** Provide a detailed list of the role's responsibilities, emphasizing the impact the role has on the supply chain's success.

3. **Qualifications:** Specify the educational background, experience, and skills required for the position.

4. **Company Overview:** Offer insight into your organization's mission, values, and culture to attract candidates who align with your ethos.

5. **Benefits and Perks:** Highlight the benefits and perks of working for your organization, such as competitive compensation, professional development opportunities, and work-life balance.

6. **Application Instructions:** Clearly outline the application process, including any required documents or assessments.

Attracting Diverse Talent

To build a diverse and inclusive team, consider the language and tone used in your job descriptions. Avoid language that may unintentionally discourage underrepresented groups from applying. Emphasize your commitment to diversity and inclusion in your job postings.

Effective Recruitment Strategies

Recruiting top talent requires a strategic approach that extends beyond posting job listings. Effective recruitment strategies encompass various methods for identifying, attracting, and evaluating candidates.

Proactive Talent Sourcing

Proactively sourcing talent involves seeking out potential candidates before you have an immediate need to fill a position. Strategies for proactive talent sourcing include:

- **Networking:** Attend industry events, conferences, and networking opportunities to connect with potential candidates.

- **Talent Pools:** Create and maintain talent pools of qualified candidates who have expressed interest in joining your organization.

- **Social Media:** Utilize professional social media platforms like LinkedIn to identify and engage with potential candidates.

Streamlined Screening and Selection

Streamlining your screening and selection process is essential to identify the best-fit candidates efficiently. Key components of an effective screening and selection process include:

- **Structured Interviews:** Develop standardized interview questions and evaluation criteria to ensure consistency in candidate assessments.

- **Skills Assessments:** Use skills assessments or tests relevant to the role to gauge candidates' abilities accurately.

- **Reference Checks:** Conduct thorough reference checks to validate candidates' qualifications and work history.

- **Behavioral Interviews:** Include behavioral questions to assess how candidates handle specific situations and challenges.

Employer Branding

Your organization's reputation as an employer plays a significant role in attracting top talent. Positive employer branding can be cultivated through:

- **Employee Testimonials:** Encourage current employees to share their positive experiences working for your organization on social media or through testimonials on your website.

- **Company Culture:** Promote your organization's inclusive and positive workplace culture, highlighting employee development, diversity, and work-life balance.

- **Professional Development:** Emphasize opportunities for career growth and professional development within your organization.

Team Development and Training

Once you've assembled a talented team, their ongoing development and training become paramount to your supply chain's success. Continuous learning and skill development ensure that your team remains adaptable and capable of meeting evolving challenges.

Individual Development Plans

Individual development plans (IDPs) are personalized roadmaps for each team member's professional growth. Key elements of effective IDPs include:

- **Goals:** Establish clear and measurable development goals for each team member.

- **Training:** Identify the training and learning opportunities required to achieve those goals.

- **Timeline:** Set a timeline for completing the development plan, including milestones and checkpoints.

- **Feedback:** Encourage regular feedback and evaluation to track progress and adjust the IDP as needed.

Cross-Training and Skill Diversification

Cross-training and skill diversification are essential strategies for building a resilient supply chain team. These practices ensure that team members can step into different roles and adapt to changing circumstances.

- **Cross-Training:** Cross-training involves teaching team members the responsibilities of other roles within the supply chain. This enables them to cover for colleagues during absences and collaborate effectively.

- **Skill Diversification:** Encourage team members to diversify their skill sets by learning new tools, technologies, or techniques relevant to their roles. This enhances their versatility and adaptability.

Onboarding New Team Members

Effective onboarding sets the stage for new team members' success within your organization. It's a process that integrates them into your team, ensures they understand their roles and responsibilities, and aligns them with your organizational culture.

Structured Onboarding Process

A structured onboarding process typically includes the following components:

- **Orientation:** Introduce new team members to your organization's mission, values, culture, and policies.

- **Role-specific Training:** Provide training that is tailored to the individual's role and responsibilities.

- **Mentoring:** Assign a mentor or buddy to help new team members acclimate to their roles and answer questions.

- **Introduction to Team:** Facilitate introductions to team members and key stakeholders.

- **Performance Expectations:** Clearly communicate performance expectations, objectives, and KPIs.

Continual Feedback and Evaluation

Regular feedback and evaluation during the onboarding process are crucial for identifying any areas where additional support or training may be needed. Encourage open communication and solicit feedback from new team members to ensure a smooth transition.

Continuous Learning and Skill Development

The supply chain and logistics landscape is dynamic, with new technologies and practices continually emerging. Continuous learning and skill development are essential to keep your team's knowledge and capabilities up to date.

Encouraging a Learning Culture

Fostering a culture of continuous learning involves creating an environment where team members are encouraged and supported in their pursuit of knowledge and skill development. Key elements of a learning culture include:

- **Access to Resources:** Provide access to learning resources, such as online courses, industry publications, and training programs.

- **Learning Opportunities:** Encourage attendance at conferences, workshops, and seminars to stay current with industry trends.

- **Skill-sharing:** Facilitate knowledge sharing within the team through peer-to-peer training and mentorship programs.

- **Recognition:** Recognize and celebrate team members' achievements and commitment to learning.

Skill Maintenance and Enhancement

Skill development is not a one-time event but an ongoing process. Encourage your team to regularly assess their skills, identify areas for improvement, and seek opportunities for skill enhancement.

Fostering Collaboration and Communication

Effective teamwork relies on collaboration and clear communication. Fostering a collaborative culture within your supply chain team is essential for tackling complex challenges and achieving shared goals.

Building a Collaborative Culture

A collaborative culture is characterized by:

- **Openness:** Encouraging open dialogue and idea sharing among team members.

- **Inclusivity:** Ensuring that all team members, regardless of their role or background, have the opportunity to contribute and be heard.

- **Problem-Solving:** Collaboratively addressing challenges and working together to find solutions.

- **Shared Responsibility:** A sense of shared responsibility for the team's success and the willingness to support one another.

Effective Team Communication Strategies

Effective communication is the cornerstone of collaboration. Employ the following strategies to enhance team communication:

- **Regular Meetings:** Hold regular team meetings to discuss goals, progress, and challenges.

- **Clear Communication Channels:** Establish clear channels for team communication, both formal and informal.

- **Active Listening:** Encourage active listening to ensure that team members truly understand one another.

- **Feedback Culture:** Create a culture of feedback where team members feel comfortable providing and receiving constructive feedback.

- **Technology Tools:** Leverage collaboration and communication tools to facilitate information sharing and project coordination.

Conflict Resolution and Management

Conflict is a natural part of any team dynamic. Effective conflict resolution and management are essential skills for supply chain leaders.

Constructive Conflict Resolution

Constructive conflict resolution involves addressing conflicts in a way that leads to positive outcomes. Key steps in constructive conflict resolution include:

- **Identification:** Identify the source of the conflict and the parties involved.

- **Active Listening:** Listen to each party's perspective to understand their concerns and motivations.

- **Objective Evaluation:** Assess the situation objectively, considering the impact on the team and the organization.

- **Mediation:** If necessary, mediate the conflict by facilitating a productive discussion between the parties involved.

- **Resolution:** Work with the parties to reach a resolution that addresses their concerns and aligns with team and organizational goals.

Conflict Management Skills

Developing conflict management skills within your team is essential for preventing conflicts from escalating and fostering a harmonious working environment. Encourage team members to:

- **Communicate Openly:** Encourage team members to express their concerns openly and respectfully.

- **Seek Common Ground:** Help conflicting parties identify common goals and interests.

- **Collaborate on Solutions:** Encourage parties to collaborate on finding solutions that benefit everyone.

- **Stay Solution-Oriented:** Emphasize the importance of focusing on solutions rather than dwelling on the conflict itself.

- **Escalation Protocols:** Establish clear protocols for escalating conflicts when they cannot be resolved at the team level.

In conclusion, building a winning team in the supply chain and logistics industry begins with talent acquisition and recruitment but extends far beyond. It encompasses team development, onboarding, continuous learning, cross-training, collaboration, and effective communication. Additionally, effective conflict resolution and management skills are essential to maintain a harmonious and high-performing team. As a supply chain leader, your ability to assemble, develop, and nurture a winning team is instrumental in achieving supply chain excellence and resilience in an ever-evolving landscape.

Diversity and inclusion (D&I) are not just buzzwords in the modern workplace; they are essential elements of building a high-performing, winning team in the supply chain and logistics industry. Embracing diversity, fostering an inclusive environment, and leveraging diverse perspectives contribute significantly to team effectiveness, innovation, and adaptability.

Embracing Diversity for Enhanced Performance

Diversity within your supply chain team encompasses differences in race, gender, age, ethnicity, sexual orientation, disabilities, and more. Embracing this diversity can lead to several benefits that enhance team performance:

Broader Skillsets

A diverse team brings a wide range of skills, experiences, and backgrounds to the table. This diversity of expertise can help your team tackle complex challenges, adapt to changing situations, and innovate more effectively.

Enhanced Problem-Solving

Diverse teams are often better equipped to solve complex problems. The inclusion of varied perspectives and approaches can lead to more comprehensive and creative solutions.

Improved Decision-Making

Diverse teams tend to make more balanced and informed decisions. Different viewpoints challenge assumptions and encourage a more critical evaluation of options.

Enhanced Adaptability

In a rapidly changing supply chain landscape, adaptability is key. Diverse teams are often more adaptable and open to change, as they are accustomed to different viewpoints and approaches.

Attracting and Retaining Talent

A commitment to diversity and inclusion can make your organization more attractive to a broader range of talent. It also fosters an environment where employees feel valued and supported, contributing to higher retention rates.

Strategies for Inclusive Leadership

Inclusive leadership is the foundation of creating a diverse and inclusive supply chain team. As a leader, your actions and behaviors set the tone for your team's inclusivity. Here are strategies for practicing inclusive leadership:

1. Lead by Example

Demonstrate inclusive behaviors in your interactions with team members. Treat everyone with respect, actively listen to their ideas, and value their contributions regardless of their background.

2. Foster a Culture of Belonging

Create an environment where every team member feels like they belong and can be their authentic selves. Celebrate diversity and make efforts to include everyone in team activities and discussions.

3. Provide Equal Opportunities

Ensure that all team members have equal access to opportunities for growth, development, and advancement. Be mindful of biases that may affect decision-making and actively address them.

4. Encourage Diverse Voices

Promote diversity of thought by encouraging team members to share their perspectives and ideas. Create forums for open dialogue and debate, where all voices are heard and valued.

5. Implement Inclusive Policies

Review and update your organization's policies and practices to ensure they are inclusive and do not inadvertently disadvantage any group. This includes policies related to hiring, promotions, and employee benefits.

6. Educate and Raise Awareness

Provide training and education on diversity and inclusion for your team. This can include workshops, seminars, and discussions that help team members understand the importance of diversity and how to be inclusive.

Leveraging Diverse Perspectives

Diverse perspectives are an asset in the supply chain and logistics industry, where complex problems often require innovative solutions. Here's how you can harness the power of diverse perspectives within your team:

1. Collaborative Problem-Solving

Encourage cross-functional collaboration within your team. When team members from different backgrounds work together, they bring diverse perspectives to problem-solving, leading to more effective solutions.

2. Diverse Project Teams

When forming project teams, consider including team members with varied backgrounds and experiences. This diversity can lead to more comprehensive project outcomes and innovative approaches.

3. Inclusive Brainstorming

During brainstorming sessions, create an inclusive environment where all ideas are welcome and valued. Avoid shutting down ideas too quickly and encourage contributions from everyone.

4. Feedback and Evaluation

When evaluating team performance, consider how well diverse perspectives were leveraged. Did the team benefit from these varied viewpoints, and if not, what improvements can be made?

5. Mentorship and Leadership Development

Identify high-potential team members from underrepresented groups and provide them with mentorship and leadership development opportunities. This helps nurture diverse talent for future leadership roles.

In conclusion, diversity and inclusion are not just moral imperatives but also strategic advantages in the supply chain and logistics industry. Embracing diversity, practicing inclusive leadership, and leveraging diverse perspectives can lead to enhanced team performance, innovation, and adaptability. As a supply chain leader, your commitment to fostering diversity and inclusion within your team can contribute significantly to achieving supply chain excellence in an ever-evolving landscape.

Chapter 5: Performance Optimization - Key Performance Indicators (KPIs) and Metrics

In the dynamic world of supply chain and logistics, optimizing performance is essential to meet customer demands, drive efficiency, and stay competitive. This chapter explores the critical role of key performance indicators (KPIs) and metrics in assessing and improving supply chain performance. We'll also delve into the impact of technology and automation, supply chain risk management, and sustainability practices in achieving excellence.

Identifying Critical Metrics in Supply Chain and Logistics

Measuring success begins with identifying the right metrics. In the supply chain and logistics context, critical metrics help you track performance, make informed decisions, and drive continuous improvement.

Types of Critical Metrics

1. **Cost Metrics:** These metrics assess the cost-effectiveness of your supply chain operations. They include:

    - Cost per order

    - Transportation costs

    - Inventory carrying costs

2. **Delivery Metrics:** These metrics measure the efficiency and reliability of your delivery processes. They include:

    - On-time delivery rate

    - Lead time

    - Order fill rate

3. **Quality Metrics:** Quality metrics evaluate the accuracy and reliability of your products and services. They include:

- Order accuracy
- Supplier quality
- Returns and defects

4. **Inventory Metrics:** These metrics gauge inventory management efficiency. They include:

- Inventory turnover
- Days of inventory on hand
- Stockout rate

5. **Customer Satisfaction Metrics:** Customer-focused metrics assess your ability to meet customer expectations. They include:

- Net Promoter Score (NPS)
- Customer satisfaction surveys
- Customer retention rate

6. **Environmental Metrics:** These metrics evaluate the sustainability and environmental impact of your supply chain. They include:

- Carbon emissions
- Energy consumption
- Waste reduction

Setting SMART KPIs

When defining KPIs, follow the SMART (Specific, Measurable, Achievable, Relevant, Time-bound) framework to ensure they are well-defined and aligned with your supply chain objectives.

Measuring Team Performance

Team performance is a critical component of overall supply chain success. Measuring and managing team performance requires a combination of quantitative and qualitative approaches.

Quantitative Metrics

1. **Output Metrics:** Quantitative measures like order processing times, order accuracy rates, and throughput can assess the efficiency and productivity of your team.

2. **Cost Metrics:** Evaluate the cost-effectiveness of your team's operations by tracking labor costs, overhead expenses, and cost per unit.

3. **Utilization Metrics:** Measure how effectively your team's resources are utilized. This can include tracking equipment uptime, employee utilization rates, and space utilization.

Qualitative Assessment

1. **Employee Surveys:** Conduct regular surveys to gather feedback from team members about their working conditions, job satisfaction, and suggestions for improvement.

2. **Performance Reviews:** Conduct performance reviews to provide individual feedback and set performance improvement goals.

3. **Team Collaboration:** Assess how well team members collaborate, communicate, and work together to achieve common goals.

Continuous Improvement through Data

Data-driven decision-making is at the core of supply chain excellence. Leveraging data analytics and continuous improvement methodologies can drive optimization.

Data Collection and Analysis

1. **Data Sources:** Identify the sources of data within your supply chain, including enterprise resource planning (ERP) systems, warehouse management systems (WMS), and transportation management systems (TMS).

2. **Data Analytics:** Employ data analytics tools and techniques to extract valuable insights from the data. This includes descriptive analytics, predictive analytics, and prescriptive analytics.

Continuous Improvement Methodologies

1. **Lean Six Sigma:** Implement Lean Six Sigma principles to reduce waste, improve processes, and enhance overall supply chain performance.

2. **Kaizen:** Embrace the Kaizen philosophy of continuous improvement, encouraging small, incremental changes and involving employees at all levels in the improvement process.

3. **Total Quality Management (TQM):** Implement TQM principles to focus on quality, customer satisfaction, and continuous improvement.

4. **Supply Chain Optimization:** Use optimization models and algorithms to make data-driven decisions regarding inventory management, demand forecasting, and transportation planning.

Technology and Automation

Technology and automation are driving forces in modern supply chains, revolutionizing the way businesses operate and optimizing performance.

The Role of Technology in Modern Supply Chains

1. **Visibility:** Technology provides real-time visibility into supply chain processes, allowing for better tracking and management of inventory, shipments, and orders.

2. **Data Integration:** Integrated technology systems enable the seamless flow of data between different supply chain functions, improving communication and decision-making.

3. **Predictive Analytics:** Advanced analytics and machine learning algorithms can predict demand, identify trends, and optimize inventory levels.

4. **IoT and Sensors:** Internet of Things (IoT) devices and sensors provide real-time data on the condition and location of goods, enhancing supply chain monitoring and control.

Leveraging Automation for Efficiency

1. **Warehouse Automation:** Automated systems, such as robotic pickers and automated guided vehicles (AGVs), streamline warehouse operations, reduce errors, and increase efficiency.

2. **Transportation Automation:** Automation in transportation includes route optimization, autonomous vehicles, and smart logistics platforms that enhance delivery speed and reduce costs.

3. **Inventory Management:** Automated inventory management systems use RFID and barcode technology to track inventory levels and trigger reorders automatically.

4. **Order Processing:** Automation in order processing speeds up order fulfillment, reduces errors, and enhances customer satisfaction.

Supply Chain Risk Management

Supply chain risk management is essential for safeguarding your operations against disruptions, ensuring business continuity, and optimizing performance.

Identifying and Mitigating Supply Chain Risks

1. **Risk Assessment:** Conduct a thorough risk assessment to identify potential risks, including supplier disruptions, geopolitical issues, natural disasters, and economic fluctuations.

2. **Risk Mitigation Strategies:** Develop strategies to mitigate identified risks. This may involve diversifying suppliers, creating contingency plans, or investing in redundancy.

3. **Supplier Collaboration:** Collaborate closely with key suppliers to understand their vulnerabilities and work together to build resilience.

Developing Resilience Strategies

1. **Resilience Planning:** Develop a comprehensive resilience plan that outlines how your supply chain will respond to various disruptions. Include scenarios for different risk factors.

2. **Business Continuity:** Establish business continuity plans that ensure essential operations can continue in the event of a disruption.

3. **Supply Chain Mapping:** Create a detailed supply chain map to identify critical nodes and dependencies.

4. **Risk Monitoring:** Implement systems for real-time risk monitoring and early warning systems.

Sustainability and Green Logistics

Sustainability is an increasingly important aspect of supply chain and logistics operations. Green logistics practices not only reduce environmental impact but also contribute to cost savings and customer satisfaction.

The Importance of Sustainability in Logistics

1. **Environmental Impact:** Logistics activities, including transportation and warehousing, have a significant environmental footprint. Sustainable practices aim to reduce this impact.

2. **Cost Savings:** Sustainability measures often lead to cost savings through reduced energy consumption, waste reduction, and more efficient operations.

3. **Regulatory Compliance:** Many regions have implemented environmental regulations that impact logistics operations. Compliance is essential to avoid penalties.

Implementing Eco-Friendly Practices

1. **Transportation Efficiency:** Optimize transportation routes, consolidate shipments, and use fuel-efficient vehicles to reduce emissions.

2. **Energy-Efficient Warehousing:** Implement energy-efficient lighting, heating, and cooling systems in warehouses and distribution centers.

3. **Waste Reduction:** Minimize packaging waste, recycle materials, and adopt sustainable packaging practices.

4. **Supplier Sustainability:** Collaborate with suppliers to ensure their sustainability practices align with your supply chain goals.

Supply Chain Carbon Footprint Reduction

1. **Carbon Footprint Measurement:** Calculate your supply chain's carbon footprint to understand the environmental impact.

2. **Emissions Reduction Strategies:** Develop strategies to reduce emissions, such as adopting cleaner transportation options or investing in renewable energy sources.

3. **Transparency and Reporting:** Communicate your sustainability efforts transparently to stakeholders and consider sustainability reporting frameworks.

In conclusion, performance optimization in supply chain and logistics hinges on the effective use of KPIs and metrics, the integration of technology and automation, robust risk management practices, and a commitment to sustainability. These elements collectively drive efficiency, agility, and resilience, allowing organizations to excel in a rapidly evolving global landscape.

Chapter 6: Leading Through Change - Managing Change in the Supply Chain

In the fast-paced world of supply chain and logistics, change is not just a constant but often an accelerator of progress. This chapter explores the essential skills and strategies for leading through change, managing industry disruptions, and fostering innovation to stay ahead in the evolving landscape.

Adapting to Industry Disruptions

The supply chain and logistics industry is no stranger to disruptions, from natural disasters to global pandemics. Adapting to industry disruptions requires agility, resilience, and proactive strategies.

Disruption Assessment

1. **Risk Assessment:** Identify potential disruptions and assess their impact on your supply chain.

2. **Supply Chain Mapping:** Create a detailed map of your supply chain to pinpoint vulnerabilities.

3. **Scenario Planning:** Develop scenarios for various disruption scenarios, including their likely consequences and response plans.

Business Continuity

1. **Business Continuity Planning:** Establish robust business continuity plans that ensure essential operations can continue during disruptions.

2. **Supply Chain Resilience:** Build resilience into your supply chain by diversifying suppliers, implementing redundancy, and securing critical supply sources.

Leading Teams Through Change

Change can be unsettling for teams, but effective leadership can guide them through transitions smoothly and with minimal disruption.

Change Leadership

1. **Vision and Communication:** Communicate a clear vision for change and the reasons behind it to inspire buy-in and enthusiasm.

2. **Empathy:** Understand and address the concerns and anxieties of team members as they navigate change.

3. **Change Champions:** Identify and empower change champions within your team who can support their colleagues through the transition.

Change Management Models

1. **Kotter's 8-Step Model:** Explore John Kotter's eight-step model for leading change, from creating a sense of urgency to anchoring the change in the organization's culture.

2. **ADKAR Model:** Learn the ADKAR model, which focuses on Awareness, Desire, Knowledge, Ability, and Reinforcement as key stages in successful change management.

Change Management Best Practices

Successful change management relies on a set of best practices that ensure a smooth transition and minimize disruption.

Planning and Preparation

1. **Change Readiness Assessment:** Evaluate your organization's readiness for change and identify potential roadblocks.

2. **Change Management Team:** Assemble a dedicated change management team to oversee the process.

3. **Communication Plan:** Develop a comprehensive communication plan that keeps all stakeholders informed and engaged.

Employee Involvement

1. **Engagement and Feedback:** Involve employees in the change process, seek their input, and provide opportunities for feedback.

2. **Training and Support:** Offer training and support to ensure employees have the skills and resources they need to adapt.

Monitoring and Adaptation

1. **Key Performance Indicators (KPIs):** Define KPIs to measure the progress and impact of the change initiative.

2. **Feedback Loops:** Create mechanisms for ongoing feedback and adjustment to address challenges as they arise.

Supply Chain Innovation

Innovation is the lifeblood of progress in the supply chain and logistics industry. Embracing innovation can lead to competitive advantages and improved efficiency.

Encouraging a Culture of Innovation

1. **Innovation Mindset:** Foster an organizational culture that encourages and rewards innovation.

2. **Idea Generation:** Provide platforms and processes for employees to contribute innovative ideas.

3. **Risk-Taking:** Create an environment where calculated risks are encouraged as part of the innovation process.

Case Studies of Innovative Supply Chain Practices: Amazon's Robotics-Powered Fulfillment Centers

Background: Amazon, the global e-commerce giant, has always been at the forefront of innovation in the supply chain industry (Amazon, n.d.). One of its most striking innovations is the implementation of robotics in its fulfillment centers. This case study explores how Amazon's use of robotics has revolutionized order fulfillment and logistics operations.

The Challenge: Amazon faced the challenge of managing an ever-increasing volume of customer orders while maintaining quick delivery times and accuracy (Amazon, n.d.). Traditional manual picking and packing processes were becoming bottlenecks in their operations, especially during peak seasons.

The Innovation: Amazon introduced an army of robots to complement its human workforce in fulfillment centers (Amazon, n.d.). These robots are part of the Amazon Robotics system, formerly known as Kiva Systems, which the company acquired in 2012. The key elements of this innovation include:

1. Automated Storage and Retrieval: Amazon's warehouses are equipped with an extensive grid of shelving units. When an order comes in, the robots spring into action. They autonomously

navigate the warehouse, locate the specific shelf containing the required product, and transport the entire shelf to a human worker for order packing (Amazon, n.d.). This reduces the time workers spend walking through the warehouse, making order fulfillment significantly more efficient.

2. Improved Accuracy: Robots have a near-perfect accuracy rate when it comes to finding and retrieving products (Amazon, n.d.). This minimizes the likelihood of errors in order picking and packing, resulting in higher customer satisfaction.

3. Scalability: As demand grows, Amazon can easily scale up its operations by deploying more robots. These robots are designed to work alongside humans, enhancing overall efficiency (Amazon, n.d.).

4. 24/7 Operation: Robots don't require breaks or rest, allowing Amazon to operate its fulfillment centers around the clock, further reducing order processing times (Amazon, n.d.).

5. Data-Driven Optimization: The Amazon Robotics system constantly collects data on the movement of products and the efficiency of operations. This data is used to continuously optimize the layout of the fulfillment center and the routing of robots (Amazon, n.d.).

Results: Amazon's innovative use of robotics in its supply chain has yielded impressive results (Amazon, n.d.):

1. Increased Efficiency: The use of robots has significantly increased the speed and efficiency of order fulfillment. This is especially crucial during peak shopping seasons like Black Friday and the holiday season.

2. Reduced Labor Costs: While robots are a substantial upfront investment, they reduce the labor required for routine tasks, ultimately saving on labor costs.

3. Enhanced Accuracy: The accuracy of order fulfillment has improved, resulting in fewer errors and fewer customer complaints.

4. Rapid Expansion: Amazon has been able to rapidly expand its fulfillment network to meet growing demand, thanks in part to the scalability of its robotic workforce.

5. Faster Delivery Times: With more efficient order processing, Amazon can offer faster delivery options like same-day and one-day shipping to customers in many regions.

Conclusion: Amazon's adoption of robotics in its fulfillment centers is a prime example of innovative supply chain practices (Amazon, n.d.). By harnessing the power of automation and data-driven optimization, Amazon has not only met the challenge of a rapidly growing customer base but has also set new industry standards for efficiency and customer service in the e-commerce sector. This case study illustrates the transformative potential of innovative technologies in supply chain management.

Please note that the specific publication date for this case study was not provided. In such cases, using "n.d." (no date) is appropriate for in-text citations.

Implementing New Technologies

1. **Technological Advancements:** Stay updated on the latest technologies shaping the supply chain, such as IoT, blockchain, and AI.

2. **Technology Integration:** Implement technology solutions that align with your supply chain goals and support your team's performance.

Future Trends and Emerging Technologies

Stay ahead of the curve by exploring future trends and emerging technologies that are likely to impact the supply chain and logistics industry.

Predicting the Future of Supply Chain and Logistics

Delve into strategies for predicting the future landscape of the industry, including scenario planning and trend analysis.

Preparing Your Team for Industry Changes

Equip your team with the skills and knowledge needed to thrive in a rapidly evolving supply chain landscape.

Continuous Adaptation and Innovation

Understand that innovation and adaptation are ongoing processes. Encourage your team to continually seek opportunities for improvement and innovation.

In conclusion, leading through change, managing disruptions, fostering innovation, and preparing for the future are all essential elements of supply chain leadership. By embracing change as an opportunity for growth and innovation, supply chain leaders can navigate industry shifts and lead their teams toward sustained success in an ever-evolving landscape.

Conclusion: Nurturing High-Performance Teams in the Supply Chain

In this concluding section, we delve into each of the four key aspects that define the concluding chapter of "Supply Chain Leadership Mastery: Crafting High-Performing Winning Teams." These aspects encapsulate the essence of effective supply chain leadership, emphasizing the importance of sustaining excellence, keeping the team motivated, recognizing accomplishments, and fostering an unwavering commitment to continuous improvement.

Sustaining High Performance and Continuous Improvement

Context: Sustaining high performance is not a one-time achievement but an ongoing endeavor in the dynamic supply chain and logistics industry. Supply chain leaders must continually seek ways to optimize operations, reduce costs, enhance customer satisfaction, and adapt to changing market conditions. This context highlights the importance of a long-term perspective in supply chain leadership.

Key Considerations:

- **Continuous Monitoring:** Regularly monitor key performance indicators (KPIs) to identify areas for improvement.

- **Feedback Loops:** Establish feedback mechanisms to gather insights from team members, stakeholders, and customers.

- **Kaizen Philosophy:** Embrace the Kaizen philosophy of continuous improvement, where small incremental changes lead to significant enhancements over time.

- **Agile Practices:** Implement agile supply chain practices that enable quick responses to market shifts and emerging opportunities.

Maintaining Team Momentum

Context: Maintaining team momentum is a critical aspect of leadership in the supply chain and logistics industry. Teams that lose momentum can become sluggish, less innovative, and less productive. It's the leader's role to ensure that the team remains motivated, engaged, and focused on achieving the organization's goals.

Key Considerations:

- **Clear Direction:** Provide a clear vision and strategic goals to keep the team aligned and motivated.

- **Recognition:** Acknowledge and celebrate the team's achievements and milestones to boost morale.

- **Professional Development:** Invest in team members' growth and development to keep their skills and knowledge up-to-date.

- **Effective Communication:** Maintain open and transparent communication channels to address concerns and share updates.

- **Empowerment:** Empower team members to take ownership of their work and contribute to decision-making processes.

Celebrating Achievements

Context: Celebrating achievements is a powerful motivator that reinforces positive behavior and performance. It fosters a sense of pride and accomplishment among team members, promoting a culture of excellence and dedication to achieving even greater success.

Key Considerations:

- **Recognition Programs:** Establish recognition programs that highlight exceptional individual and team achievements.

- **Public Acknowledgment:** Publicly acknowledge and appreciate the contributions of team members during meetings or company-wide communications.

- **Rewards and Incentives:** Offer rewards or incentives, such as bonuses or additional time off, for outstanding performance.

- **Team Celebrations:** Organize team-building events or celebrations to commemorate milestones and successes.

Commitment to Ongoing Improvement

Context: A commitment to ongoing improvement is at the heart of supply chain leadership mastery. Leaders who are dedicated to continuous learning, innovation, and adaptation are better equipped to navigate the ever-evolving supply chain landscape and drive their teams toward excellence.

Key Considerations:

- **Lifelong Learning:** Encourage a culture of lifelong learning and professional development within the team.

- **Innovation Culture:** Foster an innovation culture where team members are encouraged to propose and implement innovative ideas.

- **Benchmarking:** Continuously benchmark your supply chain practices against industry best practices and emerging trends.

- **Adaptive Leadership:** Embrace adaptive leadership practices that allow you to pivot and make informed decisions in response to changing circumstances.

In conclusion, these four aspects encompass the essence of effective supply chain leadership and team management. By sustaining high performance, maintaining team momentum, celebrating achievements, and committing to ongoing improvement, supply chain leaders can not only excel in their roles but also inspire their teams to reach new heights of excellence in the complex and ever-changing world of supply chain and logistics. As we reach the culmination of our journey through "Supply Chain Leadership Mastery: Crafting High-Performing Winning Teams," it is with a sense of accomplishment and anticipation that we reflect on the profound insights and strategies shared within these pages. We have explored the multifaceted landscape of leadership in the supply chain and logistics industry—a dynamic realm where excellence is not a destination but a continuous journey.

In our quest to master supply chain leadership, we've encountered the essential building blocks of visionary leadership, the critical importance of teamwork, and the art of performance optimization. We've examined the role of technology, risk management, and sustainability in shaping the future of logistics. We've navigated change, celebrated innovation, and embraced the ever-evolving nature of our industry.

But, most importantly, we've discovered that at the heart of it all lies the unwavering commitment to the development and nurturing of high-performing winning teams. Teams that not only meet the challenges of today but also anticipate and adapt to the demands of tomorrow. Teams that are united by a shared purpose, inspired by a common vision, and fueled by the desire to achieve supply chain excellence.

Leadership in the supply chain and logistics industry is not for the faint of heart. It requires the courage to make tough decisions, the agility to pivot in the face of adversity, and the compassion to lead with empathy. It demands an unwavering dedication to continuous improvement, a commitment to ethical practices, and a passion for fostering diversity and inclusion.

As you close the pages of this book and embark on your leadership journey—or continue the path you've been diligently treading—we invite you to carry with you the wisdom shared here. Apply the principles, embrace the challenges, and seize the opportunities that lie ahead. Remember that leadership is not a solitary pursuit; it is a collaborative endeavor that thrives when leaders and teams unite in pursuit of a common goal.

Your role as a supply chain and logistics leader is pivotal. You are the catalyst for change, the architect of strategies, and the guardian of your team's growth and success. Never underestimate the impact you can have on your organization, your industry, and the world at large.

Appendances:

Sample Team Building Exercise: "Supply Chain Simulation Game"

Objective: Enhance teamwork, communication, and problem-solving skills within your supply chain team by simulating real-world supply chain scenarios.

Materials Needed:

- A large empty space (conference room or outdoor area)

- Flipchart or whiteboard

- Markers

- Timer

- Scenario cards (prepared in advance)

Instructions:

1. **Team Formation:** Divide your supply chain team into smaller groups, ideally 4-6 members per group. Ensure that each group has a mix of roles, including procurement, logistics, warehouse, and distribution.

2. **Scenario Introduction:** Explain the objective of the exercise: to simulate various supply chain scenarios and make collective decisions to optimize the supply chain's performance.

3. **Scenario Cards:** Prepare scenario cards in advance, each describing a unique challenge or scenario that a real supply chain might encounter. Examples include unexpected demand spikes, supplier delays, transportation disruptions, or quality control issues.

4. **Simulation Rounds:** Conduct several simulation rounds, each with a different scenario. Here's how a round might work:

a. Present Scenario: Give each group a scenario card describing the challenge they must address. Be sure to include specific details, such as the nature of the problem, its impact on the supply chain, and any constraints or limitations.

b. Decision Time: Allow each group a set amount of time (e.g., 20 minutes) to discuss and make decisions on how to respond to the scenario. They must collaborate, assign roles, and determine the best course of action.

c. Presentation: Each group presents their decisions and the reasoning behind them to the entire team. Encourage discussions and questions.

d. Evaluation: Facilitate a discussion about the various decisions made by the groups. Compare the pros and cons of each approach and highlight lessons learned.

5. **Debrief:** After completing all simulation rounds, gather the entire team for a debrief session. Discuss the following:

- What were the most challenging scenarios, and how did teams address them?

- Did teams effectively communicate and collaborate?

- What strategies emerged as successful in optimizing the supply chain in these scenarios?

- Were there any innovative solutions or creative problem-solving approaches?

6. **Key Takeaways:** Conclude the exercise by summarizing the key takeaways and lessons learned. Emphasize the importance of effective teamwork, communication, adaptability, and decision-making in real-world supply chain challenges.

7. **Action Plan:** Encourage the team to brainstorm and develop an action plan for applying the lessons learned from the simulation exercise to their actual supply chain processes.

This team building exercise not only promotes collaboration and problem-solving but also provides a safe environment for supply chain professionals to practice decision-making and adaptability in a dynamic supply chain context. It helps build a stronger, more cohesive team capable of addressing real-world supply chain challenges with confidence.

Recommended Reading and Resources:

To complement the book "Supply Chain Leadership Mastery: Crafting High-Performing Winning Teams," here is a list of recommended reading and resources that cover a wide range of topics related to supply chain management, leadership, and team building:

1. "The Lean Supply Chain: Managing the Challenge at Tesco" by Barry Evans and Robert Mason

- Provides insights into how Tesco, a global retail giant, optimized its supply chain operations using lean principles.

2. "Supply Chain Management: Strategy, Planning, and Operation" by Sunil Chopra and Peter Meindl

- Offers a comprehensive overview of supply chain management, including key concepts, strategies, and practical applications.

3. "The Goal: A Process of Ongoing Improvement" by Eliyahu M. Goldratt and Jeff Cox

- A classic novel that introduces the Theory of Constraints and its application to supply chain optimization.

4. "Leaders Eat Last: Why Some Teams Pull Together and Others Don't" by Simon Sinek

- Explores the role of leadership in creating a sense of safety, trust, and collaboration within teams.

5. "Drive: The Surprising Truth About What Motivates Us" by Daniel H. Pink

- Examines the science of motivation and how leaders can foster a culture of autonomy, mastery, and purpose within their teams.

6. "Good to Great: Why Some Companies Make the Leap... and Others Don't" by Jim Collins

- Investigates the characteristics of companies that achieved sustained excellence and how leadership played a pivotal role.

7. "The Five Dysfunctions of a Team: A Leadership Fable" by Patrick Lencioni

- Explores common challenges that teams face and offers strategies for overcoming them.

8. Harvard Business Review (HBR)

- A valuable source of articles, case studies, and research papers on leadership, supply chain management, and team dynamics.

9. APICS (Association for Supply Chain Management)

- Offers a wide range of resources, including publications, webinars, and certification programs related to supply chain management.

10. MIT Sloan School of Management's Supply Chain Management Program - Provides free online courses, articles, and research on supply chain management and innovation.

11. Council of Supply Chain Management Professionals (CSCMP) - Offers research, publications, events, and networking opportunities for supply chain professionals.

12. "The Innovator's Dilemma: When New Technologies Cause Great Firms to Fail" by Clayton Christensen - Explores the challenges companies face in adapting to disruptive technologies, which is relevant to supply chain innovation.

13. "Green Logistics: Improving the Environmental Sustainability of Logistics" by Alan McKinnon - Focuses on sustainability in logistics and strategies for reducing the environmental impact of supply chain operations.

These resources cover a wide spectrum of topics relevant to supply chain leadership, team building, and continuous improvement. They offer valuable insights, best practices, and case studies to further enhance your knowledge and leadership skills in the supply chain and logistics field.

Glossary:

This glossary provides a comprehensive overview of key supply chain and logistics terminology, including terms related to supply chain technologies and the various stages of the supply chain, from first mile to final mile logistics.

1. Supply Chain Management (SCM): The strategic planning and execution of processes to ensure the efficient flow of goods, information, and finances from suppliers to end customers.

2. Logistics: The process of planning, implementing, and controlling the efficient movement and storage of goods, services, and related information from the point of origin to the point of consumption.

3. Inventory Management: The process of overseeing and controlling the ordering, storage, and use of materials or finished products to ensure a company has the right amount of stock at the right time.

4. Just-in-Time (JIT): A strategy that aims to reduce inventory levels by receiving goods only when needed for production or sales, minimizing waste and holding costs.

5. Distribution: The process of moving goods from the manufacturer to distributors, retailers, or end consumers, including warehousing, transportation, and order fulfillment.

6. Warehouse Management System (WMS): Software or technology used to optimize and automate warehouse operations, including inventory tracking, picking, and shipping.

7. Third-Party Logistics (3PL): A company that provides logistics services on behalf of another organization, often including transportation, warehousing, and distribution.

8. Procurement: The process of sourcing, purchasing, and acquiring goods, services, or materials required for a business's operations.

9. Freight Forwarder: A company or individual that arranges and manages the transportation and logistics of goods on behalf of shippers, often across international borders.

10. Bill of Lading (BOL): A legal document issued by a carrier to a shipper that details the type, quantity, and destination of goods being shipped.

11. Lead Time: The time it takes for an order to be fulfilled from the moment it is placed until it is received.

12. Cross-Docking: A logistics strategy where goods are received, sorted, and immediately shipped out to their final destination without being stored in a warehouse.

13. Demand Forecasting: The process of predicting future customer demand for products or services to ensure adequate supply and optimize inventory levels.

14. SKU (Stock Keeping Unit): A unique identifier for a specific product or item within a company's inventory.

15. Reverse Logistics: The process of managing the return of products from customers to manufacturers or distributors, often for repairs, recycling, or disposal.

16. Incoterms (International Commercial Terms): A set of internationally recognized rules defining the responsibilities of buyers and sellers in international trade, including terms like FOB (Free On Board) and CIF (Cost, Insurance, Freight).

17. Carrier: A company or individual responsible for transporting goods from one location to another, such as a trucking company, shipping line, or courier service.

18. Supply Chain Visibility: The ability to track and monitor the movement of goods and information throughout the supply chain in real-time.

19. Safety Stock: Extra inventory held to safeguard against fluctuations in demand, supply disruptions, or lead time variability.

20. Value Stream Mapping: A visualization tool used to analyze and improve the flow of materials and information in a production or supply chain process.

21. Internet of Things (IoT): A network of interconnected physical devices, sensors, and software that collect and exchange data to improve supply chain visibility and monitoring.

22. Artificial Intelligence (AI): The use of machine learning and algorithms to analyze data, optimize operations, and make informed supply chain decisions.

23. Blockchain: A decentralized and secure digital ledger technology used to enhance transparency and traceability in supply chain transactions.

24. First Mile: The initial stage of the supply chain process, which involves sourcing, procurement, and transportation from suppliers to the manufacturer or distribution center.

25. Middle Mile: The phase of the supply chain that involves the transportation and distribution of goods from the manufacturer or distribution center to regional hubs or fulfillment centers.

26. Final Mile: The last stage of the supply chain that focuses on the delivery of goods from a distribution center or hub to the end customer, often involving specialized transportation services.